J

COUNTRY PROFILES

PERU

BY ALICIA Z. KLEPEIS

BELLWETHER MEDIA • MINNEAPOLIS, MN

Blastoff! Discovery launches
a new mission: reading to learn.
Filled with facts and features, each
book offers you an exciting new
world to explore!

This edition first published in 2019 by Bellwether Media, Inc.

No part of this publication may be reproduced in whole or in part
without written permission of the publisher.
For information regarding permission, write to Bellwether Media, Inc.,
Attention: Permissions Department,
6012 Blue Circle Drive, Minnetonka, MN 55343.

Library of Congress Cataloging-in-Publication Data

Names: Klepeis, Alicia, 1971- author.
Title: Peru / by Alicia Z. Klepeis.
Description: Minneapolis, MN : Bellwether Media, Inc., 2019. |
    Series: Blastoff! Discovery : Country Profiles | Includes bibliographical
    references and index.
Identifiers: LCCN 2018039182 (print) | LCCN 2018039420
    (ebook) | ISBN 9781681036809 (ebook) | ISBN
    9781626179622 (hardcover : alk. paper)
Subjects: LCSH: Peru–Juvenile literature.
Classification: LCC F3408.5 (ebook) | LCC F3408.5 .K54 2019
    (print) | DDC 985–dc23
LC record available at https://lccn.loc.gov/2018039182

Editor: Rebecca Sabelko   Designer: Brittany McIntosh

Printed in the United States of America, North Mankato, MN.

TABLE OF CONTENTS

MACHU PICCHU

MACHU PICCHU

It is a mild, misty morning in the mountains. A family departs from the city of Cusco. After traveling for a few hours by train and bus, they reach Machu Picchu. The family wanders the **Inca** city built around 1450. They study **terraces** that were used for growing crops and explore palaces, storage rooms, and baths.

OTHER TOP SITES

CHURCH OF SAN FRANCISCO

LAKE TITICACA

MANÚ NATIONAL PARK

SANTA CATALINA MONASTERY

After wandering the ruins, they check out the Temple of the Sun. It is believed the Inca emperor lived near this temple. In the late afternoon, the family listens while hummingbird calls travel through the air. Welcome to Peru!

COLOMBIA

ECUADOR

CHICLAYO

TRUJILLO

PERU

LIMA

PACIFIC
OCEAN

CUSCO

AREQUIPA

N
W ┼ E
S

PENGUINS IN PERU!

Humboldt penguins make their home on
the Ballestas Islands. They can swim as
fast as 30 miles (48 kilometers) per hour!

CHILE

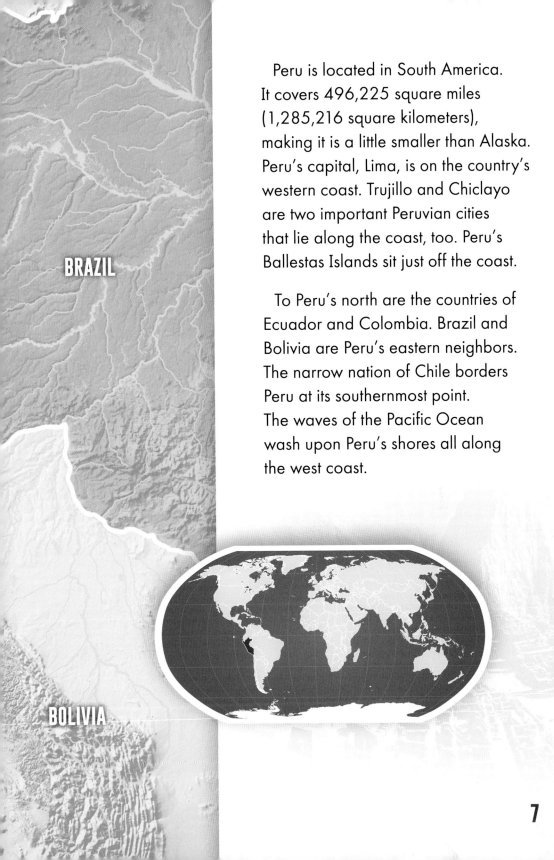

BRAZIL

BOLIVIA

Peru is located in South America. It covers 496,225 square miles (1,285,216 square kilometers), making it is a little smaller than Alaska. Peru's capital, Lima, is on the country's western coast. Trujillo and Chiclayo are two important Peruvian cities that lie along the coast, too. Peru's Ballestas Islands sit just off the coast.

To Peru's north are the countries of Ecuador and Colombia. Brazil and Bolivia are Peru's eastern neighbors. The narrow nation of Chile borders Peru at its southernmost point. The waves of the Pacific Ocean wash upon Peru's shores all along the west coast.

LANDSCAPE AND CLIMATE

The Amazon **rain forest** covers nearly half of Peru. It is home to the Amazon River that begins in eastern Peru and empties into the Atlantic Ocean. West of the Amazon forest lie the Andes Mountains, which run from north to south through Peru. A long, narrow strip of desert lines the country's Pacific coast.

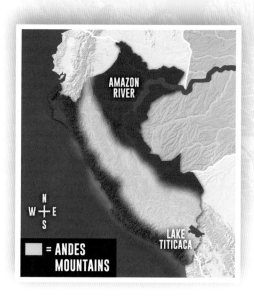

AMAZON RIVER

N
W + E
S

= ANDES MOUNTAINS

LAKE TITICACA

HOMEMADE ISLANDS

Peru and Bolivia share Lake Titicaca, the largest lake in South America. The Uros Floating Islands, made out of totora reeds by native communities, are found on the lake!

RAINBOW MOUNTAIN
ANDES MOUNTAINS

LIMA
Average seasonal highs and lows

JANUARY
HIGH: 79 °F (26 °C)
LOW: 68 °F (20 °C)

APRIL
HIGH: 76 °F (24 °C)
LOW: 66 °F (19 °C)

JULY
HIGH: 67 °F (19 °C)
LOW: 60 °F (16 °C)

OCTOBER
HIGH: 69 °F (21 °C)
LOW: 61 °F (16 °C)

°F = degrees Fahrenheit
°C = degrees Celsius

Peru has three main climates. The west coast is dry. Temperatures do not change much from season to season in this region. Mountainous areas have cooler average temperatures than the lowlands. The Amazon is hot and humid.

9

WILDLIFE

Peru has a wide variety of wildlife. South American sea lions swim in the waters off the coast as Inca terns soar in the skies above. In the Andes Mountains, guanacos eat grasses while chinchillas eat leaves, fruits, and small insects. The vicuña, Peru's national animal, also makes its home in the Andes. Brightly colored blue-moustached barbets perch on branches in the wooded highlands.

Jaguars and black caimans feed on small lowland tapirs and other animals in the Amazon rain forest. Pink Amazon river dolphins splash in the river. Enormous green anacondas also swim there, looking for prey.

CHINCHILLA

JAGUAR

VICUÑA

GIANT GREEN ANACONDAS

The Amazon is home to green anacondas. These enormous snakes are around 17 feet (5 meters) long. The largest are more than 33 feet (10 meters) in length. Some weigh up to 550 pounds (249 kilograms)!

BLUE-MOUSTACHED
BARBET

BLUE-MOUSTACHED BARBET

Life Span: unknown
Red List Status: least concern

blue-moustached barbet
range =

LEAST CONCERN	NEAR THREATENED	VULNERABLE	ENDANGERED	CRITICALLY ENDANGERED	EXTINCT IN THE WILD	EXTINCT

Over 31 million people live in Peru. A little less than half are **native** Americans. Their **ancestors** are originally from Peru. The second-biggest group is *mestizos*. They are **descendants** of the native people and Europeans. Other Peruvians have European, African, Japanese, and Chinese ancestors.

Most Peruvians belong to the Roman Catholic Church. Others practice different kinds of Christianity. Some practice a mixture of **traditional** and Christian beliefs. Peru has three official languages. They are Spanish, Quechua, and Aymara. Around four out of every five Peruvians speak Spanish. Quechua and Aymara are native languages.

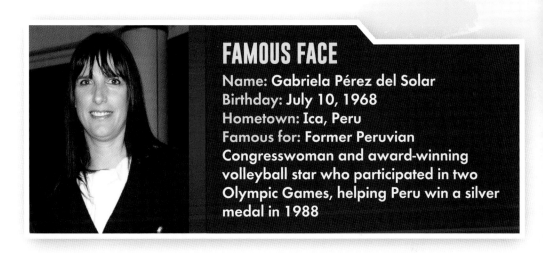

FAMOUS FACE

Name: Gabriela Pérez del Solar
Birthday: July 10, 1968
Hometown: Ica, Peru
Famous for: Former Peruvian Congresswoman and award-winning volleyball star who participated in two Olympic Games, helping Peru win a silver medal in 1988

SPEAK SPANISH

ENGLISH	SPANISH	HOW TO SAY IT
hello	hola	OH-lah
goodbye	adiós	ah-dee-OHS
please	por favor	pohr fah-VOR
thank you	gracias	grah-SEE-ahs
yes	sí	SEE
no	no	noh

LIMA

Most Peruvians live in **urban** areas. Some people live in high-rise apartments or in houses. But many people in Lima live in **slums**. Homes are made from whatever materials are available. City travel is often by bus.

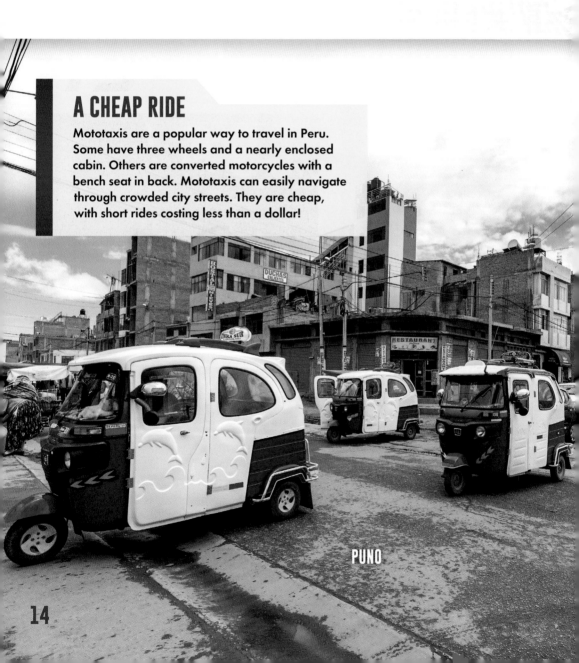

A CHEAP RIDE

Mototaxis are a popular way to travel in Peru. Some have three wheels and a nearly enclosed cabin. Others are converted motorcycles with a bench seat in back. Mototaxis can easily navigate through crowded city streets. They are cheap, with short rides costing less than a dollar!

PUNO

ADOBE HOUSES
TAQUILE ISLAND

In the countryside, homes are commonly built from **adobe**. People in **rural** areas usually travel by foot or by using animals. Families in Peru often have several children. About half of Peruvians live with extended family members. Newly married adults often live with their parents briefly after their wedding. Elderly people commonly move in with their children.

People in Peru use a lot of hand gestures when talking. They stand close and make constant eye contact while speaking with others.

In cities, people often wear Western-style clothing. But in the countryside, people commonly wear brightly colored, handwoven, traditional clothing related to their **ethnic** group. Women might wear several colorful skirts, a sweater, and sandals called *ojotas*. Men wear colorful ponchos with patterns that tell which region they are from. Peru is known for the *chullo*, a wool hat with ear flaps that tie under the chin. *Chullos* often feature images of native animals.

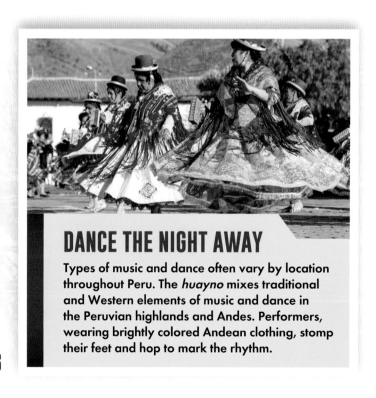

DANCE THE NIGHT AWAY

Types of music and dance often vary by location throughout Peru. The *huayno* mixes traditional and Western elements of music and dance in the Peruvian highlands and Andes. Performers, wearing brightly colored Andean clothing, stomp their feet and hop to mark the rhythm.

Children in Peru attend six years of primary school. They typically start around age 5. Next comes five years of secondary school. Wealthier families may send their children to private Catholic schools. These offer a wider variety of courses than most public schools. Students who complete secondary school can attend universities.

About one in every four Peruvians works in agriculture. Farmers grow coffee beans, fruit, asparagus, and other vegetables. Over half of the workforce have **service jobs**. They work in schools, hotels, and offices. Other Peruvians **manufacture** products like machinery or clothing.

MANUFACTURING CLOTHING

FARMER

MONEY FROM POOP

Peru is the world's leading producer of *guano*, or bird poop. The word comes from the Quechua word *huanu*, meaning "dung." The country exports guano to nations around the globe to use as fertilizer on farms.

VOLLEYBALL

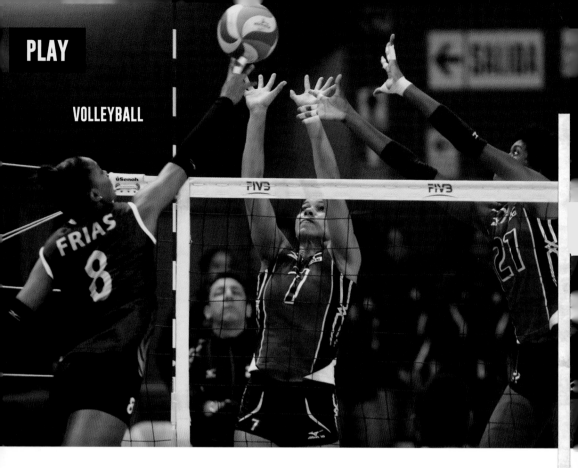

The most popular sport in Peru is *fútbol*, or soccer. In villages and big cities, Peruvians of all ages play. People also love to watch matches between Peru's many professional soccer teams. Peruvians enjoy volleyball and tennis, too. The national women's volleyball team has been successful at competitions around the world. Surfing and hiking are common as well.

FÚTBOL

Peruvians like socializing in their free time. Modern and traditional dancing are popular. Many people watch soap operas called *telenovelas* for fun. People also go to the movies for entertainment.

PERUVIAN PANPIPES

Panpipes are a popular traditional instrument in the Andes Mountains of Peru.

What You Need:

- 8 plastic straws
- ruler
- scissors
- tape

Instructions:

1. Cut the straws so you have one of each of the following lengths: 2, 2 1/2, 2 3/4, 3, 3 1/2, 3 3/4, 4, 5 inches (6, 6 1/2, 7, 8, 9, 9 1/2, 10 1/2, 12 1/2 centimeters)

2. Lay a piece of tape with the sticky side up on your work surface.

3. Arrange your straws in order from shortest to longest. Place them in order on top of the sticky side of the tape.

4. Place another piece of tape, sticky side down, on top of the straws. This will keep your flute together.

5. Play your new panpipes!

FOOD, NOT PETS

Guinea pigs are a traditional food in Peru. People serve them crispy and with their heads still on!

Potatoes, corn, and white rice are **staples** of the Peruvian diet. **Tropical** fruits are also enjoyed. People often eat bread and butter with jam or ham for breakfast. Potato soup is common in the colder highland areas. A popular lunchtime dish is *papa a la huancaína*, a baked potato with sliced eggs and sauce.

Dinner might be leftovers or bread with meats and cheeses. Fish and different types of seafood are popular in coastal areas and the Amazon region. A popular dish is *ceviche*, spicy peppers and **marinated** raw fish. A common dessert is *picarones*, donut-like treats made from sweet potato flour.

PAPA A LA HUANCAÍNA

CEVICHE

ARROZ CON LECHE

Ingredients:
1 1/2 cups water
1/2 cup long-grain white rice (uncooked)
1 cinnamon stick
1 cup sweetened condensed milk
1 cup evaporated milk
2-3 tablespoons raisins

Steps:
1. Put the water, rice, and cinnamon stick into a small saucepan. With the help of an adult, bring to a boil, then reduce the heat. Cook uncovered over low-medium heat until the water is absorbed. This will take about 15-20 minutes.

2. Add in both milks and raisins. Bring to a boil, then reduce heat. Simmer, uncovered, until the mixture is creamy and thick. Stir it often while it simmers. This should take about 10-15 minutes. Get rid of the cinnamon stick.

3. Serve your rice pudding warm or cold.

Many Christian holidays are celebrated across Peru. *Semana Santa*, or Holy Week, is the week before Easter. People in Ayacucho celebrate with folk dancing, art shows, and horse racing. Christmas Eve, known as *La Noche Buena*, is a lively and eventful night. Many attend church services before fireworks light up the sky.

Peruvians celebrate their country's independence from Spain on July 28 and 29. Live music, dancing, and fireworks are part of the fun. Military parades and political speeches are also common. But Peruvians celebrate their **culture** and country all year long!

SEMANA SANTA

FESTIVAL OF THE SUN

On June 24, some Peruvians celebrate the ancient Inca festival *Inti Raymi,* or the Festival of the Sun. This holiday marked the beginning of the New Year in the Inca calendar.

INTI RAYMI

1824
Peru gains independence from Spain

1533
Francisco Pizarro's Spanish troops defeat the Incas

1879–1883
Peru fights the War of the Pacific with Chile and Bolivia

AROUND 1450
Incas build Machu Picchu

1854
President Ramón Castilla ends slavery in Peru

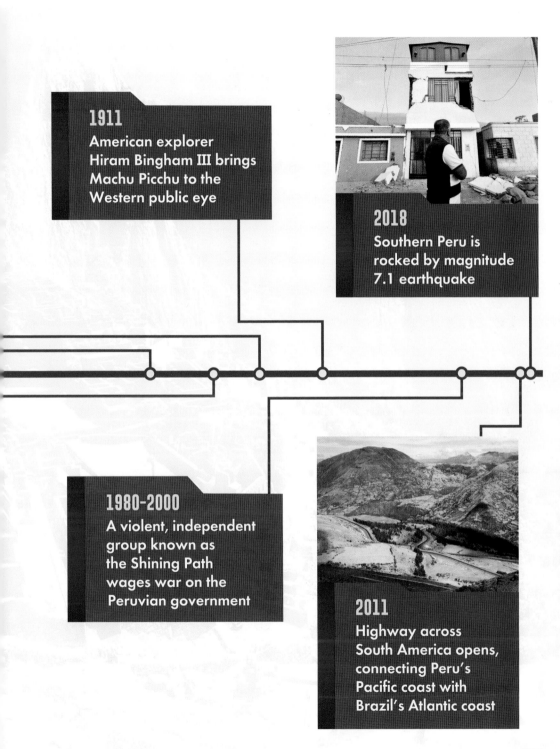

1911
American explorer Hiram Bingham III brings Machu Picchu to the Western public eye

2018
Southern Peru is rocked by magnitude 7.1 earthquake

1980-2000
A violent, independent group known as the Shining Path wages war on the Peruvian government

2011
Highway across South America opens, connecting Peru's Pacific coast with Brazil's Atlantic coast

Official Name: Republic of Peru

Flag of Peru: Peru's flag has three vertical bands of color. The left and right bands are red, representing the blood shed during the fight for independence. The central band is white, symbolizing peace. The country's coat of arms is in the middle of the white band. It includes a shield with a vicuña, a cinchona tree, and coins spilling out of a horn. This stands for the nation's mineral wealth.

Area: 496,225 square miles
(1,285,216 square kilometers)

Capital City: Lima

Important Cities: Arequipa, Trujillo, Chiclayo

Population:
31,036,656 (July 2017)

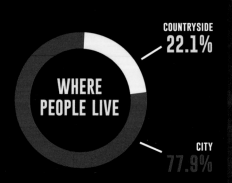

WHERE
PEOPLE LIVE

COUNTRYSIDE
22.1%

CITY
77.9%

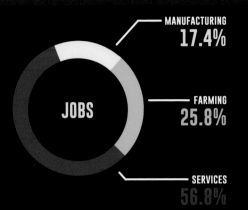

MANUFACTURING
17.4%

JOBS

FARMING
25.8%

SERVICES
56.8%

Main Exports:

copper

gold

petroleum

clothing

coffee beans

fruits and vegetables

National Holiday:
Independence Day, July 28 and 29

Main Languages:
Spanish, Quechua, Aymara

Form of Government:
presidential republic

Title for Country Leader:
president

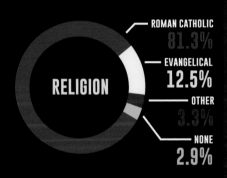

RELIGION

ROMAN CATHOLIC
81.3%

EVANGELICAL
12.5%

OTHER
3.3%

NONE
2.9%

Unit of Money:
Nuevo sol

GLOSSARY

adobe—a building material or brick made from a sun-dried mixture of straw and earth

ancestors—relatives who lived long ago

culture—the beliefs, arts, and ways of life in a place or society

descendants—people related to a person or group of people who lived at an earlier time

ethnic—related to a group of people who share customs and an identity

Inca—a native American people of Peru who maintained an empire until the Spanish conquered them

manufacture—to make products, often with machines

marinated—soaked in a sauce to enrich the flavor of food

native—originally from the area or related to a group of people that began in the area

rain forest—a thick, green forest that receives a lot of rain

rural—related to the countryside

service jobs—jobs that perform tasks for people or businesses

slums—parts of cities that are crowded and have poor housing

staples—widely used foods or other items

terraces—flat ridges on a hillside that help keep the soil in place

traditional—related to customs, ideas, or beliefs handed down from one generation to the next

tropical—related to the tropics; the tropics is a hot, rainy region near the equator.

urban—related to cities and city life

TO LEARN MORE

AT THE LIBRARY

Bjorklund, Ruth. *Peru*. New York, N.Y.: Cavendish Square, 2016.

Burgan, Michael. *Peru*. New York, N.Y.: Children's Press, 2018.

Stine, Megan. *Where Is Machu Picchu?* New York, N.Y.: Penguin Workshop, 2018.

ON THE WEB

FACTSURFER

Factsurfer.com gives you a safe, fun way to find more information.

1. Go to www.factsurfer.com.

2. Enter "Peru" into the search box.

3. Click the "Surf" button and select your book cover to see a list of related web sites.

INDEX

The images in this book are reproduced through the courtesy of: saiko3p, front cover, p. 8; vitmark, pp. 4-5; Christian Vinces, pp. 5 (top), 9 (bottom), 21 (top); insideout78, p. 5 (middle top); Prisma by Dukas Presseagentur GmbH/ Alamy, p. 5 (middle bottom); blutack, p. 5 (bottom); David Ionut, p. 9 (top); PhotoMagicWorld, p. 10 (left); Kuznetsov Alexey, p. 10 (top); milosk50, p. 10 (middle); LABETAA Andre, p. 10 (bottom); Pete Oxford/ Minden Pictures, p. 11; Allik, p. 12; ASSOCIATED PRESS/ AP Images, p. 13 (top); Igo Dymov, p. 13 (bottom); Simon Mayer, p. 14; SL-Photography, p. 15; Paulo de Abreu, p. 16; hadynyah, p. 17; National Geographic Image Collection/ Alamy, pp. 18, 27 (bottom); PixieMe, p. 19 (top); imageBROKER/ Alamy, p. 19 (bottom); EFE News Agency/ Alamy, p. 20 (top); sunsinger, p. 20 (bottom); Photo Oz, p. 21 (bottom); Bob Pool, p. 22; yasuhiro amano, p. 23 (top); Cameron Whitman, p. 23 (bottom); Brent Hofacker, p. 23 (bottom); HUGHES HervÃ© / hemis.fr/ Getty Images, p. 24; Roberto Epifanio, p. 25; Amable-Paul Coutan, p. 26 (top); PRISMA ARCHIVO/ Alamy, p. 26 (bottom); STR/ Contributor/ Getty Images, p. 27 (top); Glyn Thomas/ Alamy, p. 29 (currency); Andrey Lobachev, p. 29 (coin).